Original title:
Waves on the Horizon's Edge

Copyright © 2025 Creative Arts Management OÜ
All rights reserved.

Author: Atticus Thornton
ISBN HARDBACK: 978-1-80587-445-4
ISBN PAPERBACK: 978-1-80587-915-2

## Chasing the Born of the Breeze

A seagull stole my sandwich,
It flew off with a smirk,
As I chased it down the shore,
I tripped on a crab's work.

The wind said, 'Catch me if you can!'
I laughed and rolled my eyes,
It swirled around my head,
Like a mischievous surprise.

Footprints made a silly dance,
As I jumped and twirled,
Each step a new adventure,
In this sandy, silly world.

With friends all laughing loud,
While crabs clapped with glee,
We made our funny stories,
By the vast and salty sea.

## Beyond the Gentle Crest


A turtle tried to surf today,
It wore a tiny hat,
But every wave it conquered,
Just left him feeling flat.

We built a castle high and proud,
Only to watch it fall,
The tide came in with laughter,
Like it knew us after all.

A fish swam by with flair,
And winked at us so sly,
It knew of secret treasures,
That sparkled from the sky.

So we danced along the coast,
With jellyfish in tow,
Who knew the creature's shimmy,
Would make the sandbanks glow?

## Dreams of the Ocean's Embrace

A crab is hosting a party,
With snacks and drinks galore,
But when I tried to join the fun,
I slipped right on the floor.

The dolphins made a splashy joke,
As they leaped up so high,
But missed their landing perfectly,
With a flop and silly sigh.

Seashells whispered stories old,
To squids who danced with cheer,
While seaweed played the banjo,
In tunes we couldn't hear.

I joined the wild parade of fish,
Wiggling 'neath the sun,
And thought this dream of laughter,
Is truly just pure fun.

**Veils of Water and Sky**

A seagull with a crown of foam,
Tried to rule the ocean blue,
But slipped right off its sandy throne,
And had a royal boo-boo.

The sun played tag with passing clouds,
While I rolled in the sand,
Sunburned and giggling with joy,
Like I was in a band.

My friends dared to make a splash,
But landed in a pile,
Laughter echoed all around,
With every silly smile.

Together we raced the tides,
In a contest of pure jest,
With the ocean's endless laughter,
Making memories the best.

## **Retreating into Serenity's Grasp**

In the sand, I dig my toes,
Chasing crabs, oh how it goes!
Seagulls swoop with cheeky flair,
Stealing snacks, who even cares?

The sun dips low, a golden blob,
My hat's a ship, it starts to bob.
Friends laugh loud, a silly cheer,
Life's a joke when skies are clear!

The surf forms lines as if to tease,
I stumble, grin, 'I'll take that breeze!'
Oh, the ocean, such a prank,
Turns my thoughts to fishy rank!

As I splash in sudden bliss,
The tide pulls back, an ocean kiss.
I flail and giggle, caught off guard,
What a ride! Life's never hard!

## The Drifting Veil of Evening's Tide

The sunset paints the sky with cheer,
A cotton candy dream appears.
With flip-flops on, I dance so wild,
Like a carefree, giggling child.

The breeze whispers secrets, oh so sly,
Seagulls gossip as they fly by.
I challenge one to a race,
Forget the prize, just pick up pace!

Laughter fills the salty air,
As jellyfish float, unaware.
With seaweed wrapped like fancy bow,
I strut like royalty - what a show!

As twilight falls, the stars align,
Each one sparkles, a wink divine.
I'll toast to nature with a cup,
To silly moments, let's lift up!

## Rhapsody of the Thundering Surf

A crab in a tux, what a sight,
Dancing with joy, holding on tight.
Seagulls wear shades, strutting around,
While sandcastles crumble, they spread joy profound.

With waves like hiccups, they rise and fall,
They giggle and splash, like kids at the mall.
A fish in a bow tie sways in delight,
Proposing to driftwood under moonlight.

The ocean's a jester, a playful prank,
With jellyfish juggling, and whales in the tank.
Each splash a chortle, each crash a cheer,
In this carnival tide, there's nothing to fear.

The surf sings a tune of addled delight,
While crabs hold a concert, into the night.
As shells become maracas, and laughter prevails,
The beach is a fairground, where fun never fails.

## Underneath the Gleaming Expanse

Under the sun, the sand starts to dance,
Seashells audition for their big chance.
A starfish dreams of Hollywood fame,
While a dolphin plays chess, it's all just a game.

The sun's wearing sunscreen, with a big grin,
As foam gives a giggle, and whispers of sin.
A sea cucumber tiptoes, trying to sneak,
Wearing a tutu, looking quite chic.

The gulls tweet their selfies, quite out of line,
While octopuses argue over the best wine.
With crabs as the judges, it's chaos at sea,
Where laughter and silliness flow wild and free.

Mermaids throw parties with magical flair,
Casting their nets, with glitter in the air.
Beneath this expanse of a playful day,
The ocean's a stage, where we all want to stay.

## Where Earth Meets the Sea

On the shore where sand tickles toes,
A clam tells a joke, everyone knows.
A pelican swoops, steals a hot dog,
While a lazy old turtle lies blissfully in fog.

The gulls gather round, keen for the show,
As crab dominoes fall, one after the slow.
The surf gives a clap, in this madcap land,
With laughter so big, it stretches the sand.

Each splash is a giggle, so hearty and bright,
As fish wear balloons, adding to the light.
A sea cucumber does a hula dance,
Inviting the stars to join in their prance.

Where earth meets the ocean, silliness reigns,
The tide's a parade, with no need for chains.
With every new ripple, a chuckle erupts,
In this land of humor, where joy never stops.

## Horizons Drenched in Glistening Dreams

A pirate ship sails, with a rubber duck crew,
They're off to find treasure, just pretending, it's true.
With maps made of candy, they laugh and they play,
Even sharks in sunglasses join the ballet.

The beachcomber's bucket is filled with fine gems,
Like bottle caps, candy, and glimmering hems.
As tides toss a fortune, golden and sweet,
We dance with sea otters, a whimsical beat.

Bubbles rise high, reaching up for the sun,
While seaweed confetti floats down, what fun!
Cap'n Seagull squawks, "A toast to the tide!"
In this realm of mirth, we're all free to glide.

As horizons glisten, the giggles resound,
In this world full of joy, true love can be found.
Underneath the shimmer, let laughter be our theme,
For each day at the shore is a magical dream.

## The Hidden Dance of Nature's Rhythm

The seas prance like a silly goose,
Dancing with the breeze as their excuse.
Crabs tap their claws in a tiny ballet,
While jellyfish jiggle in a goofy display.

The seagulls squawk like they own the show,
Flapping around with a flamboyant glow.
Even the sand has a ticklish fit,
As footprints wander and then quickly quit.

Nature laughs in the sun's bright pool,
With fish predicting fortune, like a fool.
And the tides throw parties all night long,
While shells hum the ocean's silly song.

**Songs Carried by the Wind**

The wind whistles tunes with a cheeky grin,
Tickling the leaves with a playful spin.
Clouds float by like they're at a fair,
Trading cotton candy for a dash of air.

Squirrels rap on branches with a funky beat,
While ants march in rows, oh so neat!
The grass dances in skirts of emerald hue,
Laughing aloud as the sky paints blue.

A chorus of frogs joins in the cheer,
Singing to stars that flicker near.
While echoes of giggles tickle the shore,
As mother nature opens her fun-filled door.

**Celestial Kinship with the Sea**

The moon winks at the briny crew,
As stars dive in to join the view.
Shells play hide and seek with the sun,
While sea urchins giggle, having fun.

Light bulbs glow in the deep sea glee,
Chatting with fish on a make-believe spree.
A surfboard lounging with a cheeky flair,
Says, 'Catch me if you dare!' in the salty air.

Starfish stretch like they're on a quest,
Searching for laughter, the ultimate jest.
And dolphin pranks have become routine,
In this oceanic circus, oh so keen!

**Tracing the Skies Above the Abyss**

Kites dance like dolphins up in the blue,
Painting the sky with a bright, bold hue.
Birds practice somersaults with flair,
While lovers giggle beneath their care.

Clouds, soft pillows, dream on above,
Whispering secrets about the sea's love.
Even the thunder taps out a beat,
While rain drops in rhythm, oh so sweet.

The horizon jests with every twirl,
As nocturnal stars start to unfurl.
In this amber glow where giggles reside,
Everything's a dance with nature as our guide.

## Crystalline Futures Beyond the Surf

A jellyfish floats, oh what a sight,
It dances and flops, in morning light.
Seagulls squawk loudly, quite the fuss,
Stealing my fries, those feathered bus!

The sun shines bright, all golden cheer,
I trip on a shell, and it feels quite queer.
A crab waves hi with a sideways strut,
Looks like it's off on a beach bum cut!

Sunscreen greased, I slip and slide,
Chasing a kid on a colorful ride.
Sandcastles collapse with a big splat,
The king of the beach? Guess that's just that!

As sunset paints the waves pink and blue,
I spot a fish wearing a hat, it's true!
With laughter and joy, the day unwinds,
In crystalline futures, fun is what binds.

## Glimmers of Hope in the Distance

A dog on a surfboard steals the show,
He barks at the sea while catching a flow.
Kids chase ice cream, sticky sweet treat,
Can I trade my towel for just one lick? Neat!

The sand feels warm beneath my bare feet,
I dare a flip, oh isn't that neat?
But gravity's mean with a laugh and a plop,
I'm face-first in powder, it's hard to stop!

Flip-flops are flying, what a wild ride,
As friends toss beach balls with carefree pride.
We're creatures of laughter, afloat in delight,
With glimmers of hope, we dance through the night.

The sun dips slowly, colors all blend,
Time to share jokes before we descend.
With giggles and grins, we steal the day,
In this surreal sea, we'll forever play!

## The Enchanted Meeting of Elements

The sun and the sea had a quirky chat,
They argued and laughed, 'bout who's where it's at.
A breeze chimed in, with a swoosh and a swirl,
Tickling my nose, oh what a whirl!

Clouds began drawing, pictures so funny,
One looked like a duck, while another like honey.
Lightning struck joyfully, crackling with glee,
"Rain down some giggles!" it shouted with glee!

The moon joined the party, with a wink and a grin,
"Dance with the tides and let the fun spin!"
Stars twinkled brightly, casting wishes of cheer,
"Join us, dear earthlings, we'll all disappear!"

Elemental friends in a delightful clash,
Creating a carnival, a jubilant bash.
With waves dancing wildly, the night feels grand,
In the enchanted meeting, all join hand in hand.

## Ciphers Written in Sand and Foam

Footprints in sand tell tales of delight,
Of kids running freely from morning to night.
Shells whisper secrets of oceans afar,
While crabs play hopscotch; they're stellar by far!

Frogs in the tide pools practicing hops,
They joke with the seaweed, who answers their props.
A starfish flips over, showing its rays,
"Who knew this life could be such a maze?"

Foam curls like laughter, it dances and jigs,
It teases the shells as it frolics and digs.
Tiny fish parade, with scales all aglow,
They wink as they pass, putting on quite a show!

With each ebb and flow, stories emerge,
Ciphers in sand, they invite us to urge.
So laugh with the tide, with the sun overhead,
In this silly ocean, we happily tread.

## Awakening the Silent Abyss

The ocean snores, what a strange sight,
A crab wearing socks, oh what a delight!
Fish do a jig, under the moon's glow,
While seagulls debate, on where to go.

Shells play the flute, with a soft sway,
Starfish dance wildly, in their odd ballet.
The tides giggle softly, as they tease the shore,
And clams tell jokes, oh what a roar!

## The Last Light Before Darkness Falls

The sun waves goodbye, gives the sea a kiss,
As dolphins conspire, in a splashing bliss.
A lighthouse winks, with a cheeky grin,
While night sends in crabs, ready to begin.

A starfish plays poker, with a sly charm,
While jellyfish float, causing some alarm.
Seaweed performs magic, twisting with flair,
As the ocean's laughter fills the salty air.

## Beyond the Limit of Senses

Octopuses juggle, in their colorful coats,
While turtles recite, in suave little notes.
The sand tickles toes, as they shimmy on by,
Aquatic shenanigans, beneath the blue sky.

Squid do a tango, with pirouettes grand,
As fish wear top hats, a sight truly bland.
The coral cracks jokes, in layers so bright,
Creating a carnival, in the pale moonlight.

**Echoes of Serenity in the Surf**

The ocean hums softly, like a sly little cat,
With shells doing stand-up, fancy that!
Barnacles gossip, about barnacle wives,
While lobsters ponder, the meaning of lives.

A whale makes a splash, with a belly laugh,
As seals breakdance, in their own little half.
The tide takes a bow, in a dramatic way,
And sea foam joins in, for an end of the day!

## Tides of Distant Dreams

A jellyfish wearing a hat,
Dances like a rhythmic brat.
It sings a tune with flair and glee,
While seagulls sip their cups of tea.

A crab in shades walks with style,
Strutting proudly for a while.
He trips and tumbles in the sand,
Announcing jokes that make us stand.

A starfish reads a comic book,
While turtles give the ocean a look.
They laugh at tales of fishy pranks,
And plan their trips to hidden banks.

The sun dips low, the sky's turning red,
As fish rehearse a laugh-filled thread.
They tickle tides with silly cheer,
Making dreams float ever near.

## Whispering Currents Beneath the Sky

An octopus braids its long hair,
While crabs gossip without a care.
They trade seashells in cheerful tones,
And build a castle of silly cones.

Dolphins wear their sparkly ties,
Flipping high as they crack wise.
"Who needs land?" they chortle proud,
As they perform in front of a crowd.

A clam recites a corny jest,
While fish swarm in a flashy fest.
With fins they wave, they shimmy and shake,
For a laugh is all it takes.

Under the stars, the fun won't cease,
As playful tunes bring endless peace.
The sea's alive with giggles and roars,
A laughter that echoes from ocean floors.

## The Sea's Embrace at Twilight

A whale wears shoes to make a splash,
While dolphins all do a crazy dash.
They flip and twist, a grand parade,
In waters where all worries fade.

A fish in a bow tie sings so loud,
While sea cucumbers form a crowd.
"Let's throw a party, turn the tide!"
They dance around, bursting with pride.

Crabs play poker on the sandy floor,
With shells as chips and laughter galore.
The stakes are high, the giggles even,
As they jive under the sky's soft beacon.

At twilight's hour, they caper and twirl,
In a world submerged, where joy does unfurl.
With every splash, the sea's sweet refrain,
Keeps our spirits light, just like champagne.

## Ripples of Tomorrow's Secrets

A fish with glasses reads the news,
While plankton throw a quirky blues.
With gossip swirling in the brine,
They trade tall tales and drink fine wine.

A seagull plays the ukulele,
While snails move slow, but oh so daily.
They gather close, a merry band,
As laughter spills upon the sand.

A crab conducts the laughter choir,
While tides hum tunes that never tire.
They weave a rhythm, who could guess,
That secrets hide in sandy dress?

The moonlight winks, the fun won't end,
As creatures start to twist and bend.
In a sea of dreams, bright hopes collide,
Rippling secrets swell with pride.

## Eclipsed by the Vastness of Blue


I planned a grand day by the sea,
But forgot my sunscreen, oh woe is me!
My nose now a beacon, bright and bold,
As laughter erupts, my fate is foretold.

The seagulls squawk, a comical crew,
They dive for my chips, as if on cue.
I swat at the air, flailing around,
While they snatch my lunch from the ground.

A crab joins the party, with a sidestep so sly,
He clicks at my toes, I can't even cry.
I wish for a towel, to hide from the show,
But the ocean just laughs, as it steals my glow.

## The Heart of a Rolling Current

In the surf, I spotted a fish with a hat,
He winked at the sun and chatted with that.
With bubbles of laughter, he swam to and fro,
And I just sat there, enjoying the show.

A wave gave a push, and I fell to my rear,
I giggled so hard, I might disappear.
The finned friend chuckled, a real jester he,
As I splashed right back, like a child carefree.

The tides hold secrets, or so they insist,
I'll write them a letter, they'll get the gist.
For every big laugh inside gales that grow,
I'll dance with the sea, with a tickle and flow.

## A Tapestry Woven by the Deep

The ocean's a quilt, with patches that tease,
Each ripple a story, floating with ease.
A jellyfish wobbles, with style and flair,
While a clam tells a joke, I can't help but stare.

I tried to impress with a flip or a dive,
But ended up splashing, all flailing alive.
The fish gathered round, for my comedy show,
With scales all a-twinkling, they laughed to and fro.

A dolphin, quite suave, twirled in the brine,
"Your antics, my friend, are genuinely fine!"
With a wink and a flip, the party began,
As we danced through the surf, like a catchy jam.

**The Soft Call of Nature's Hand**


The wind rustles gently, a playful decree,
Whispers of laughter drift in the sea.
I chase after shadows, a fool on the run,
Only to trip on sand, oh this is fun!

An octopus winks, with a leg full of grace,
Says, "Join in the chaos, let's pick up the pace!"
I stand in confusion, with a laugh and a spin,
The soft call of nature feels like a win.

We'll ride on the breezes, with giggles and cheer,
With seashells as trophies, we'll shout, "Mama, here!"
For in this grand folly, we hardly step back,
With joy as our compass, we're on the right track.

**Light's Dance on the Water's Breath**

The sun donned its sparkly attire,
And slipped on the dance floor of blue,
Fish in tuxedos, quite inspired,
Twirl to a song they all knew.

Seagulls in shades, a fancy crew,
Critique the moves of the fish parade,
"Oy, that one's off-beat," they coo,
While diving for snacks — not afraid!

Crabs tap their claws in rhythm anew,
With their pinch-perfect steps, how they prance!
Barnacles boast, "We're stuck like glue,"
Yet they cheer and join the wild dance!

So when you feel life is a bore,
Just look to the sea, and you'll find,
A party awaits on the ocean floor,
Where laughter and splashes unwind.

## **Boundless Horizons Await**

There's a llama on a surfboard, it seems,
Trying to catch the swell with some flair,
He's dreaming of tropical ice cream,
While getting his hooves tangled in air!

The turtles throw a luau at noon,
Inviting the dolphins for snacks,
They all take a dip to a catchy tune,
In the middle of their silly acts!

The sun wearing shades, laughing with glee,
As crabs spin tales of their lost socks,
The tide tickles toes with salty decree,
Creating a friendship that rocks!

So grab your board and join the fun,
Life's better with giggles, not threats,
Embrace the horizon, the journey just begun,
Take a leap, and forget your regrets!

## Faraway Whispers in the Salt Air

There's a duck in a boat, telling tall tales,
To fishes who giggle, flipping their fins,
"Aliens took my last pair of scales!"
While seagulls roll eyes, munching on bins.

A crab tells a story, all shiny and bold,
Of treasures found in a giant's beard,
"Don't judge my whiskers, they're worth their gold!"
The audience cheers, having no fears.

The whispering breeze plays its tune,
With echoes of laughter, light and airy,
The stars peek down, "Who will dance soon?"
The seashells respond, "Oh, let us be scary!"

So next time you stroll by the shore,
Listen close to the silly galore,
For faraway whispers of laughter,
Are what salt air's truly made for.

## The Language of Distant Shores

On distant sands, the crabs have a chat,
In a tongue made of claps and twirls,
"Did you see the otter in that tall hat?!"
He'll juggle some seaweed and pearls!

Mermaids splash tales of fishy delight,
As they sip on coconut cream,
The dolphins giggle, dancing in sight,
Finding the world a humorous dream.

The sun paints the sky with colors so rich,
While turtles on surfboards try to glide,
One flips and yells, "Oh, what a hitch!"
They laugh as they crash — what a ride!

So listen to the tales of the ocean's embrace,
Where laughter and sounds freely blend,
For every splash holds a smile on its face,
And the mystery dances till the end.

## The Infinite Blue Beckons

In the distance, a splash and a glide,
A seagull wears a fishy side.
The ocean laughs with a bubbly cheer,
While I slip on sand, oh dear, oh dear!

Sunburned noses, a sight to see,
Chasing crabs like they're on a spree.
Sandcastles claim their sandy throne,
But they fall like dreams, oh how they moan!

The jellyfish dance with flappy flair,
While beach balls soar through salty air.
A flip-flop flies, a fitting song,
And someone shouts, "Where did I go wrong?"

Laughter echoes, the tide and tease,
As gulls dive down with utmost ease.
Handstands topple like waves o'er board,
In this sandy saga, life's never bored!

## Embracing the Incoming Light

Sunshine spills like lemonade,
As sunscreen battles can't be delayed.
My friend is yellow, a true hotshot,
   While I resemble a lobster pot!

The sky's a stage for clouds that twirl,
A sea breeze makes my hair unfurl.
Dancing shadows, a playful spree,
As flip-flops march in bizarre glee!

I spotted a mermaid, or was it a seal?
She winked at me; what a surreal deal!
We chat about sand and sun-protected skin,
   Hoping my sunscreen will finally win.

The shine of the water steals the show,
As I swear my towel just said hello!
With giggles and splashes, we embrace the glare,
In the warmth of the light, nothing can compare!

## When the Sea Meets the Sky

Fishing boats drift with a goofy start,
A crab in a boat?! Now that's an art!
The clouds conspire with hues so bright,
While seagulls squawk and take flight!

An octopus trickles with eight-legged grace,
Playing tag in this splashing space.
A dolphin leaps with acrobatic flair,
As I dive in, not a worry or care!

Beach towels spread like a colorful quilt,
Ice cream drips—akimbo and spilt!
A sandcastle stands but crumbles so sweet,
While kids look for treasures at their sandy feet.

Picnic lunches filled with strange combos,
Tuna and jelly? Where did that go?
As the sun dips down with a glittery show,
I'll pack up laughter from this wild flow!

## Coastal Serenade

With a plop and a splash, the fun begins,
A fish throws a party with bubble wins.
Shells sing songs of faraway lands,
While I try to catch them with both my hands!

A lighthouse winks like a cheeky chap,
While kids chase dreams in a sandy trap.
An old crab scuttles with knowing flair,
As seagulls perform in mid-air without care.

Finding sand dollars, what a delight!
But they vanish like dreams in the night.
A kite takes off, tangled with glee,
Making the weak-hearted flee from the sea.

From sunsets painted in hues of fun,
To silly dances in the golden sun.
Let's gather the stories that tickle our souls,
In this coastal tale where laughter rolls!

## **Tidal Echoes of Forgotten Tales**

Once a crab danced in the sand,
Claiming to be a rock star band.
With claws on his drum, he'd play away,
Until the tide came for a buffet.

Fish told jokes, they swam so fast,
Their punchlines made the seaweed laugh.
One fin slipped, a fish did glide,
Into a sea cucumber with pride.

A dolphin wore a sailor's hat,
Claiming he was better than a cat.
He tried to sing a shanty loud,
But only made the octopus proud.

Seagulls flew with silly glee,
Stealing fries from kids by the sea.
They squabbled, cawed, in a food race,
All for a chance to steal a taste.

## Beneath the Veil of Emerald Waters

A clam once held a beauty pageant,
Judged by fish who claimed to be gallant.
But the sea cucumber stole the show,
With slime and a wink, he said hello!

Turtles surfed on jellyfish waves,
While shrimp wore ties and misbehaved.
One dared to dance on a whale's back,
And got soaked in a watery snack.

Squid in bow ties, what a sight,
Throwing ink while trying to fight!
They slipped and slid in their inky mess,
Turning the ocean into a dress.

Anemones swung on the seabed floor,
As crabs clapped like they wanted more.
The party raged beneath the tide,
With laughter echoing far and wide.

## The Silent Voyage of a Dream

Bubbles floated like dreams set free,
A fish said, 'I once dreamed of tea!'
With a kettle made of coral bright,
He brewed a storm, oh what a sight!

A starfish tried out for a role,
In a play of the deep, oh what a goal!
But with arms too stiff, he missed his cue,
And flopped like a fish that never flew.

The sea horses galloped in a race,
In tiny tuxedos, such a silly space.
They giggled as they splashed about,
Turning serious seas into a shout.

Then came a whale with a loud wheeze,
Trying to imitate the gentle breeze.
But all he did was shake the sea,
And the fish all swam away with glee.

## **Lullabies from the Deep**

In the quiet deep, creatures sang,
A puffer fish puffed as he twanged.
Turtles hummed with a graceful glide,
While octopuses kept the beat inside.

Seahorses whispered tales of old,
Of ships made of jelly and treasures of gold.
A shrimp with a mustache told a tale,
About chasing dreams without fail.

A slow-motion crab did a funny jig,
That made the clownfish laugh, oh so big!
As a wave rolled in, they took a bow,
And all agreed, 'We'll do that now!'

From the coral homes came a gentle hum,
A lullaby soft, 'til morning comes.
In the depths they dream with a giggle and grin,
Where laughter echoes, and fun begins.

## Nautical Serenade of the Soul

In boats with hats so dapper,
The fish all cheer and clap,
As sailors dance a merry jig,
And tip their mugs with a clap.

The seagulls squawk a happy tune,
From high above they take their flight,
While fish below join in the fun,
A splash, a flip, a silly sight.

The compass spins in drunken glee,
As anchors float and sails get stuck,
Each sailor hums a loony song,
And says, 'Just wait! We'll have some luck!'

With jellyfish wearing party hats,
The sea's a place of sheer delight,
With laughter rolling on the tide,
We sail into the starry night.

## **A Canvas of Celestial Tides**

Upon the sea, the stars do twinkle,
While mermaids pour their drinks with flair,
The dolphins dance with silly flips,
And laugh until they lose their hair.

The moon, a disco ball so bright,
Reflects in waves that giggle sly,
As boats go bobbing, hands in air,
To catch the fish that swim on by.

A crab in boots does shuffle by,
Declaring he's the king of cool,
While octopuses knit their socks,
In funky patterns for the school.

The universe is painted bold,
With colors that make pirates sing,
Join us on this funny ride,
And laugh with joy as oceans ring.

## Where the Light Meets the Deep

In waters deep where shadows play,
The fish wear suits and dance away,
While glowing jellyfish take flight,
And disco balls reflect the light.

A treasure chest, a silver shoe,
With goldfish doing a waltz for two,
The barnacles clap in tune so loud,
Inviting all the sea to crowd.

The depths hold secrets, weird and wild,
Where clam-shells giggle, free and mild,
And seaweed sways to jazzy grooves,
While dolphin friends show off their moves.

Laughter bubbles in salty air,
As creatures gather everywhere,
Join in the fun, it's quite a leap,
Where silly dreams stir in the deep!

## Salted Whispers of the Twilight Air

With salt on lips, the sun dips down,
The sailors swap their biggest tales,
Of fish so big they took their boat,
And ran away with all the sails.

Beneath the sky, so vast and wide,
The crabs throw parties on the shore,
While sandcastles are full of snacks,
Where seagulls scheme for tasty more.

The sun's last wink, a golden tease,
As shrimp wear shades and strike a pose,
With tidal pools that laugh and splash,
And seaweed dresses in bright clothes.

In twilight air, the giggles flow,
With salty whispers everywhere,
The ocean's pulse, a funny dance,
Invites us all to join the fair.

## The Subtle Call of Distant Shores

A seagull squawks, it's calling me,
With a voice like nails on wood, oh dear!
I pack my snacks, my trusty hat,
But forget my shoes; I'm quite the brat!

The sand tickles toes, warm as toast,
I trip on a crab, who's quite the boast.
Crabby friends, with claws all aglow,
Chuckle at me, their favorite show!

A bucket fills with shells and glee,
As the tide rolls in, I'm on a spree.
I dance like fish, in my rainbow shorts,
The beach ball answers, "Yes, of course!"

So here I stand, with sunburns bright,
"A hot dog, please!" I shout, in delight.
The distant echoes, a playful tease,
As I savor my snack, protected by seas!

## Murmurs of Celestial Waters

The ocean sighs, a tune so sweet,
Mermaids gossip, with not a care,
They sip their tea, from seaweed cups,
And I can't help but laugh, what's fair?

A dolphin spins, a circus act,
While turtles race for the best snack.
"Catch me! Catch me!" says one bold chief,
They flail and flop; it's comic relief!

A wave rolls in, my hat flies off,
I chase it down while the sea lions scoff.
"Is that your crown, oh sandy king?"
As I bow and trip, oh what a fling!

Bubbles pop, and laughter swells,
With every splash, our joy compels.
So let's rejoice in this watery show,
With gregarious fish, in the undertow!

## **Starlit Reflections on Liquid Glass**

The moonlight dances, tipsy and bright,
While fish wear shades, a silly sight.
Jellyfish boogie, oh what a scene,
With glowing costumes, they steal the sheen!

A catfish jokes, winking a fin,
He tells the tales of what's hiding within.
"Watch out!" they warn, "not all is bliss,"
As I step in, and feel the 'splash kiss!'

Sea stars sparkle, they're stars of the sea,
One says, "Dancing's for you, not for me!"
They sneak away, to create a fuss,
While crabs engage in a freestyle thus!

So here I am, beneath the show,
With slippery tales, and giggles to grow.
A starry night, so fun and bright,
Where each shimmer reflects pure delight!

## Shadows of the Past Beneath the Waves

Old ships whisper, with tales so grand,
Of pirates, treasure, and grains of sand.
But under the surface, the humor flows,
As fish recount, their sea-life woes!

A clam with pearls, thinks he's a star,
While snails boast slow, and race from afar.
"Who's the fastest?" they challenge with glee,
But slow and steady, is how it will be!

With barnacles stuck, on the hulls they cling,
They gossip and chirp, of the joy they bring.
"Was that a whale's sneeze?!" they chuckle and play,
As bubbles erupt, like laughter's ballet!

And as I listen, to stories unique,
The ocean's charm, it's silly, not bleak.
In depths below, where shadows dance,
There's humor galore in this underwater chance!

## A Journey to the Mystic Shore

I packed my bag with a rubber duck,
But the sea thought otherwise, what a luck!
My sandals flew, they took to the air,
While I stood there, a startled stare.

The seagulls laughed as I ran around,
Chasing my hat that was ocean-bound.
The tide pulled in, with a sneaky grin,
'Welcome to chaos!' it seemed to win.

I tried to surf with a pool noodle,
Instead, I danced like a wild poodle.
My friends took photos, they couldn't resist,
'Is this a beach trip or a comedy twist?'

As the day ended, I fell asleep,
Listening to giggles in waves that seep.
I'll tell the tale at the next big bash,
When life gives you tides, make a splash!

## Lighthouses and Wandering Stars

I gazed at the lighthouse, so tall and neat,
But tripped on a pebble, fell at its feet.
The light it flashed, a beacon so grand,
While I just rolled like a washed-up band.

The stars above twinkled, shared a laugh,
As I fought with my sandwich, a snack mishap.
Mayonnaise flew, on an unsuspecting crow,
'Is this a picnic or a slapstick show?'

The lighthouse keeper waved, chuckling soft,
Said, 'Your dance moves could lift you aloft!'
While I stumbled and tumbled, it became quite clear,
They'd prefer I surf on the back of a deer.

So I waved goodbye to the stars on high,
With a wink and a giggle, I let out a sigh.
For lighthouses glow, but who needs that flair,
When laughter's the light that we all can share!

**Fading Footprints on Azure Shores**

My footprints faded in the silky sand,
Like secrets whispered by a playful hand.
But when I turned, oh what a sight!
My toes were now buried, oh what a fright!

I chased a crab, it danced and darted,
While all my beach plans promptly departed.
It waved its claws in a cheeky jest,
'You call that running? Just do your best!'

The sun was shining, my towel took flight,
Landed on a sunbather, what a delight!
They sat up shocked, eyes wide with surprise,
As I burst out laughing, little sea spies.

With fading footprints and memories shared,
I'll tell this tale, 'cause I was unprepared.
For on those shores, with a giggle or two,
Every little slip makes the fun feel new!

## When Dreams Meet the Liquid Dawn


At dawn's first blush, I yawned with glee,
Then slipped on the deck, like a clumsy bee.
The tea I spilled flew in a wild arc,
While my cat leaped up, oh what a spark!

The waves whispered secrets, soft and spry,
While I fished for my shoes, oh my, oh my!
They floated away, with such carefree glee,
'Fishy business,' they chuckled, 'just wait and see!'

As sunlight danced on liquid dreams,
I fancied I heard the ocean's memes.
With each wild attempt to catch what was near,
I created a show, the crowd full of cheer.

So here's to the mornings, when clumsiness reigns,
Where laughter and splashes wipe out our pains.
For in every blunder, a new story's drawn,
When our dreams collide with each liquid dawn!

## Treading Water in a Sea of Possibilities.

I tried to surf on a rubber duck,
But it quacked back, oh what bad luck!
It paddled left while I went right,
Splashing feebly, what a sight!

Seagulls laughed, my swim was strange,
Chasing driftwood, I felt deranged.
Treading water, my feet like lead,
Dreaming of snacks, all thoughts of dread.

The tide pulled in with a cheeky grin,
I gulped some water, let the fun begin!
A crab waved its claw, with a wink,
"Join my dance!" I smiled, then I sank!

A dolphin joined, doing the twist,
"Is this how humans do?" it smirked, couldn't resist.
I flipped and flopped, what a clumsy show,
Who knew the sea was for a fashion flow?

## Whispers of the Distant Sea

The ocean whispered, tales so tall,
Of fish in suits at a fancy ball.
They danced and twirled, quite the affair,
While I dropped my sandwich, lost in despair.

Jellyfish strutting in bright puffs,
Boasting their style, all sparkling and tough.
I tried to join, but tripped on my fin,
And landed nose-first in a sea of gin!

A whale chimed in, "You've got some moves!"
But my sea legs faltered, swaying like grooves.
With a wink and a flash, it swam past me,
Leaving me tangled in kelp, feeling free!

As night fell down, I gave a bow,
To the fish in tuxes, I wondered how.
"Next time, friends!" I hollered with glee,
They just flicked their tails, and swam from me!

## **Echoes in the Misty Surf**

In the misty surf, I found a shell,
Listening close, it began to yell!
"Stop eating sand, it's way too bland!
Try shrimp cocktail, or potato planned!"

I laughed aloud at the seaside joke,
Then fell flat on my face—a slippery poke.
The tide pulled back, no sympathy there,
As crabby onlookers began to stare!

Echoes of laughter filled the cool air,
Fish in sunglasses, they really don't care.
I splashed around, and I gave them a show,
"Just part of the act!" I cried with a bow.

With every tumble, my spirits soared,
Each splash and giggle, I couldn't be bored.
And as I rose, dripping with joy,
The sea became life's ultimate toy!

## Reflections of Twilight Tides

At twilight's glow, the sea shone bright,
I danced with shadows, a whimsical sight.
Reflections stared, wearing silly hats,
Pretending to be wise, but were really just brats.

The fish giggled, a school of delight,
As I tripped on sand, losing my fight.
"Try the conga!" they called out to me,
But I mumbled, "Ain't that for a Glee?"

With every wave came a joke to tell,
Even the seagulls joined in, oh so swell!
With squeaky voices, they croaked a rhyme,
"Don't worry, mate! Dancing's all about time!"

As night crept in, stars began to wink,
The ocean chuckled, "Just stop and think!
Life's not a race, take it easy, dear,
And dance with the tide, it's all about cheer!"

## Sublime Horizons Before the Storm

The seagulls squawk, they plan a feast,
A picnic's bait, a bread roll beast.
Surfboards lined, they wait in queue,
While jellyfish enjoy their view.

Clouds gather round, they're in a huddle,
The sky's a soap opera, an endless muddle.
A single raindrop starts the dance,
As umbrellas pop up, like a silly chance.

Giggles echo as we dodge the tide,
A battle royale, we cannot hide.
Fishy pranks from flounders below,
As laughter drifts with a breezy flow.

So let the tempest come our way,
We'll chuckle and splash and surely play.
In nature's chaos, we'll find our bliss,
Each bobbing moment, a watery kiss.

## The Infinite Pulse of the Ocean's Heart

The tide rolls in with a cheeky grin,
A crab in flip-flops joins the din.
He struts with flair, casting his spell,
While starfish gossip, oh what a tale!

Bubbles burst in a giddy cheer,
Surfing pelicans lend an ear.
They have jokes, but nobody cares,
As they brave the surf with their silly airs.

The ocean plays its greatest hit,
With swells that make you laugh and sit.
A dolphin jumps in a splashing show,
Exchanging winks with the peaks below.

With every ebb, a chuckle shared,
The sea's a jest, and we're all paired.
So join the party, don't miss the fun,
In this ocean dance, we all are one.

## Shifting Sands of Time's Tapestry

In buckets bright, our castles grow,
Though seagulls plot their stingy show.
They eye our snacks with crafty glee,
As time, it slips like sand to sea.

Sandy toes and funny hats,
A game of chase with crabby brats.
My sunscreen's thick, I look like cheese,
But laughter roars upon the breeze.

Each grain a story, a giggle past,
With sandcastles made that seldom last.
The tide rolls in like a cheeky glance,
And we all join in for the next big dance.

So gather round for a sandy jest,
In shifting sands, we feel our best.
For time is funny, a twist and turn,
In every moment, new joys we learn.

# **Radiance at the Edge of Dusk**

As twilight creeps, the piers awake,
A fisherman's joke, a slippery flake.
His fishing line pretends to sing,
While an old boat dances on a swing.

Fireflies twinkle like stars in fright,
Spilling giggles through the night.
We roast marshmallows, a sticky treat,
As raccoons plot their midnight feat.

The sunset blushes, an orange hue,
While dolphins leap, prancing anew.
The moon pops out, a shy debut,
With waves of laughter in its view.

So here's to night, let's raise our cheer,
With silliness rolling, year after year.
In twilight's charm, we'll dance and play,
As the world hugs us in its gentle sway.

## **Breath of the Infinite Blue**

A fish wore a tie, so neat and so fine,
He swam to a party, feeling divine.
But the crabs got the dance floor all tied in a knot,
And poor Mr. Fish just stood there to squat.

The jellyfish boogied, all lit up in glee,
With tentacles waving, oh what a sight to see!
But Mr. Fish tripped, oh what a disgrace,
He landed right in the punch, oh, what a place!

The seagulls above just cawed with delight,
As the fish found a way to take off and take flight.
With a splash and a wink, he left them in cheer,
And vowed to avoid punch for at least another year!

So let the tides roll, and laughter still reign,
In the sea's wild party, there's never a strain.
For even the fish, with their fancy attire,
Find joy in the chaos, and dance 'round the fire!

## Silent Watches from the Shore

The lighthouse flickered, its light spinning round,
While the seagulls held gossip of what they had found.
A crab with a monocle strutted with pride,
Claiming he knew where the sea turtles hide.

The kids by the shore drew castles of sand,
And one tiny wave just laughed, saying, 'I'm grand!'
It knocked down the towers, left chaos and fuss,
As the children all shouted, 'You're making a mess!'

In the silence of sunset, they made silly faces,
As the tide playfully left funny old traces.
With seaweed adorned crowns, they reign in their play,
While all of the fish swim the other way!

As night fell upon them, stars started to twinkle,
The light from the shore made the water just wrinkle.
And on this fine night, with laughter galore,
The ocean just grinned, who could ask for more?

## Where Light and Shadow Merge

In twilight's embrace, two shadows did meet,
One tall and one short, with rather large feet.
They danced in the light, a comical sight,
As the sun dipped below, and the stars came to light.

Mr. Shadow on the left wore a hat with a flair,
While Mrs. Shadow swayed, flipping her hair.
'Your foot's in my way!' squeaked Mr. with frown,
'You're stepping on my toes—oh, please, settle down!'

But laughter erupted, as shadows rolled wide,
They twirled and they spun, like a fun, bumpy ride.
With giggles and wiggles, the dance never ceased,
Turning light into laughter, that's how joy increased.

As dawn started breaking, the shadows took flight,
Bound for the sunrise, oh what a delight!
With antics and tumbles, they promised to stay,
For where light meets the dark, there's always a play!

## The Charms of Undulating Currents

In the currents of blue, a dolphin took flight,
With a splash and a twist, oh what a delight!
He called to his friends, 'Come join in the fun!'
But the porpoise just giggled, 'Not under the sun!'

A turtle, quite wise, with a shell painted bold,
Said, 'Let's race those currents, let our tales be told!'
With a flipper and flicker, the contest began,
But who would have guessed, the starfish can ran!

Beneath the warm surface, hidden treasures await,
Like a seaweed parade, oh isn't that great?
But the seahorse just chuckled, 'I'll swim with finesse,'
While the fish made a splash in full fancy dress!

So join in the flow, find the giggles and glee,
In the charms of the currents, where we all can be free.
For life's but a dance in this shimmering sea,
With laughter and joy, come and swim here with me!

## Reflections at the Water's Threshold

The sea is a mirror, or is that my hair?
My reflection, a creature, with one less layer!
I giggle at seagulls, so proud and so loud,
As they squawk their odd verses, drawing quite a crowd.

A crab waved hello while I tripped on the sand,
With a tumble and splash, I just couldn't withstand.
He chuckled, I think, with a claw in his hand,
Telling me humor was part of the plan.

Kids build a fortress, but it's made of sea foam,
A king made of sand, declares this is home!
The tide rolls in quickly, with a mischievous grin,
Their castle's a puddle—and now we begin!

So here at the shore, with a splash and a cheer,
We frolic, we fumble, and maybe a tear.
Each moment a giggle, a tale we can share,
In this watery kingdom, where laughter's the air.

## The Solitude of the Sandy Expanse

A lone flip-flop stares, abandoned and sad,
Its partner lost somewhere, now that's really bad!
The sun, like a spotlight, on a beach bum's plight,
As he suns himself bright, in an overly tight.

The seashells have gossip, oh, what do they say?
About folks who sunbathe and loathe their own play.
With a sprinkle of sunscreen, the struggle is real,
As they slather and smear with a comedic zeal.

A sandcastle crumbles, no royal decree,
As the tide claims its throne and declares victory.
The children all weep, but I can't help but grin,
For the ocean's a joker, letting chaos begin.

So here in the solitude, smiles flicker and play,
A dance of the awkward, in the sun's warm ray.
As I chuckle alone, at this seaside affair,
In this quirk of the universe, laughter fills the air.

## Emotions Carried by the Tide

The tide rolls in softly, like a cat with a purr,
But my sandwich floats off—who knew it could stir?
A seagull swoops down, with a cheeky little squawk,
As I wrestle my lunch, oh, what a silly walk!

The ocean holds secrets, or so I have heard,
Like the mermaid who lost her favorite word.
With a splash and a giggle, her treasure went free,
Now she's stuck with a 'W,' not a 'sea.'

With every swell, my laughter does rise,
As sand nibble crabs do a dance in disguise.
They pinch and they dance, oh, what a delight!
These crustacean comedians steal hearts with their bite.

So I float with the humor, and let my joy glide,
On emotions that play with the ebb and the tide.
For each joyful moment, I'll cherish and keep,
In this laughter-filled world, where the sea is so deep.

**Passages through Coastal Memories**

With memories woven in the breeze so light,
I stumble upon treasures, like my left sock's flight.
The sand tickles toes, as I wander and roam,
Collecting these moments, yeah, I call them home.

Distant laughter echoes, like seashells in hand,
As I stumble on flip-flops, no one understands.
A child's bright balloon floats off, oh, what fun!
It's all in the name of a good beachy run.

The salt in the air laughs, tickling my nose,
As I dive into snapshots of life's little prose.
Each spade full of sand, a tale yet to tell,
Whispers of giggles ring out from the swell.

So I'll cherish this journey, both silly and grand,
As each splash and laugh helps me understand.
That life's like the ocean, vast and profound,
Filled with funny moments and joy all around.

## Dances of Liquid Light

The sea does a jig, with a splash and a twirl,
As fish wear their hats, and the seaweed gives a whirl.
Crabs do the cha-cha, in a line on the sand,
While seagulls gossip, chirping, quite unplanned.

Bubbles float by, with a fizzy delight,
Jellyfish jigging in their own glowing light.
A dolphin attempts a fancy new move,
But tumbles and laughs—oh, it's hard to groove!

Starfish are judging with critical eyes,
While barnacles rock with their weathered disguise.
The ocean's a dance floor—a splashy affair,
Where laughter and giggles drift through the air.

The tides keep the beat, as they rise and they fall,
The sea creatures sway, having quite the ball.
So join in the fun, let your worries take flight,
On this briny stage, where all is just right.

## Currents through the Stillness

A brook takes a nap, under sunbeam's embrace,
But restless old turtles are winning the race.
The water's so sneaky, it giggles and flows,
While otters wear hats, striking silly poses.

The rocks poke their heads out, all covered in moss,
Just trying to eavesdrop, but at what cost?
A frog in a tuxedo leaps with great flair,
While fish pass the news—did you see that pair?

A cormorant's gossiping, teasing out loud,
As minnows just shiver, dreaming of crowds.
The stones hold their breath, in anticipation,
For the bubbling echo of fish celebration.

Currents are sneaky friends, always in jest,
With playful intentions, they never let rest.
So tiptoe with glee, let the laughter be bright,
In the stillness we find the current's delight.

## **Shoreline Reveries**

The sand has a secret, it tickles my toes,
As crabs throw a party, wearing bright bows.
The seagulls are swooping, doing loops in the air,
While turtles are lost, with not much to spare.

Driftwood is nodding, it's wise and it's old,
While shells play the trumpet, gleaming like gold.
The sandcastles rise, with moats made of dreams,
But waves play the trickster, bursting at seams.

A beach ball's a hero, rolling with style,
Dancing with children, making them smile.
The sun winks with laughter, its rays full of cheer,
As the tide tells a story only we can hear.

So gather your joy, let your spirit unfold,
Embrace little wonders, as life becomes bold.
In the line of the sea, where fun finds its play,
We savor sweet moments, come join in the fray!

## Azure Aspirations

Floating about, on a sailboat of dreams,
With fish in top hats, plotting grand schemes.
The sky's holding meetings, with clouds in a row,
While a parrot's reciting a funny old show.

Seashells wear glasses, playing wise like a sage,
While dolphins juggle jokes, taking center stage.
A jellyfish marches, with flair and with grace,
While sea cucumbers cheer, in their gooey embrace.

The ocean's horizon, a canvas of fun,
Where sea creatures mingle, and bask in the sun.
They tip their fine hats, raising laughter galore,
In this grand azure dreamscape, forever explore.

So let's ride the currents, on waves full of cheer,
With laughter as currency, let joy persevere.
In this vibrant ocean, let's sway, spin, and dive,
For in the heart of the sea, we come truly alive.

## Echoes from the Coastal Mirage

A crab wore a hat, quite absurd,
He strutted around, oh how he spurred!
The seagulls laughed, took a dive,
For a fashion show, they planned to strive.

The ocean whispered tales of their dance,
While fish in the sea eyed the prance.
A jellyfish twirled, causing such flair,
As barnacles clapped, without a care.

Sandcastles stood with a regal pose,
But a wave snickered, "Here comes my toes!"
An octopus giggled, ink in the air,
As starfish joined in, without a care.

So next time you wander along the shore,
Look for the laughter and the playful roar.
Nature's a jester with a cheeky grin,
Where silliness thrives, and joy rushes in.

## The Dance of Water and Light

A dolphin wore shades, oh what a sight,
He flipped and he flopped in pure delight.
Sunbeams chased him, a merry crowd,
As fish in the sea cheered all aloud.

A clam started singing an off-key tune,
While turtles grooved under the bright noon.
A school of minnows brought pops and snaps,
Each wave seemed to join in, giving claps.

Crabs joined the beat, clicking their claws,
And snails breaking dance, with no pause.
The pier echoed laughter far and wide,
As sea creatures boogied with joy and pride.

So come take a sip of this fun-filled spree,
Where water and light dance wild and free.
With every splash and shimmer bright,
Nature holds a party, a true delight!

## **Lullabies of the Dusk's Drift**

As sun bids adieu, the waves hum a tune,
Seagulls croon softly, under the moon.
Starfish yawn wide, they whisper and sigh,
While fishes dream of clouds in the sky.

A crab told a tale of a treasure most rare,
Though it turned out to be just an old shoe pair.
The tide playfully rolled, teasing the sand,
As the moonlit militia danced hand in hand.

Shells sparkled bright, each glowing with fear,
Of waves that giggled, "We might just come near!"
A sea cucumber questioned, "What time is this?"
As laughter erupted in the ocean's abyss.

So drift on the lullabies, lulled by the breeze,
Where quirky sea folk do as they please.
In twilight's embrace, they sing with delight,
Crafting sweet memories in the fading light.

**Surfacing in the Shimmering Glow**

A pufferfish bloated, he thought he'd be cool,
Playing hide and seek in the water pool.
But to everyone's shock, he got stuck in a net,
As laughter erupted, oh what a pet!

An eel with a hat, dancing sideways,
Twisting and turning in charming displays.
Bubblefish giggled, rolling on by,
With giggly bubbles that reached for the sky.

Starfish held hands, practicing a chain,
Posing for selfies, but lost their gain.
The seaweed cheered, with a jiggly sway,
Turning the ocean into a grand ballet!

Then nightfall arrived, all twinkling and bright,
As everything sparkled under the moonlight.
So raise a shell high, let laughter flow,
In the waters so bright, with joy we'll bestow!

www.ingramcontent.com/pod-product-compliance
Lightning Source LLC
Chambersburg PA
CBHW060146230426
43661CB00003B/590